Dragon's La...

Campsite

Fairy Rings

Waterfall

Wishing Well

Archery Field

N

W

E

S

Also by R.C. Lloyd:

Chronic Defiance
The Cruelty of a Door

R.C. Lloyd also appears in:

Unconventional Love: Anthology on the Expanse of Love
Unleash the Cosmos: A Space Poetry Anthology

Also from Dragon Heart Press

Unleash the Cosmos: A Space Poetry Anthology
When One World Ends, Another Begins
by Nathaniel Luscombe
Tending Clay; Unearthing Stars by MJ Anthony
Best Cat in Show by Sage Evergreen

"Thistle Heart Home is a gripping collection of life's journey of belonging. Its emotional storytelling portrayed through poetry will have you pondering your own path and encouraging you to forge ahead. Lloyd's words touch the soul and tug on the heart, reminding you of who you are."

Sara Francis, author of *The Waiting Trilogy*

"R.C. Lloyd crafts a vivid and enchanting journey through her poetry. Thistleheart Home is the perfect autumnal read."

Erin Forbes, author of the *Fire & Ice* Series

"'And under the stars, all at once your mother's prayers return to you.' ThistleHeart Home was a poetic journey through nature and humanness that left me with the smell of divinity and mountain wind in my hair. A beautiful read for anyone who has ever felt lost."

Sara Rian, author of *Loving the Gone* and *Then Death Came*

"Dropped into the heart of a whimsical forest, Thistleheart Home draws the reader into depths of thought, emerging in resilience with unmatched imagery and intuitive perception. Like a lantern, this work lights a path of hope."

Feroza, singer and songwriter

THISTLEHEART
HOME

R.C.Lloyd

To my Brothers / Parents / Grandparents
My Light / My Compass / My Home

Dear Reader,

My grandmother wrapped me in prayers
A shawl to keep me safe

My mother lit a lantern
Taught me how to nurture the light

My grandpa taught me how to find the North Star
Encouraged me to follow truth

My dad builds cairns to tell the mountains he was there
Taught me to build a life

My brothers make bridges to help each other cross streams
Help me cross through fears

I named my car Atlas
In an epoch when I felt lost

My family is one of direction. We keep each other on the path, carry each other when one is weak, and chart our way by the true light.

"Your word is a lamp to my feet and a light to my path." Psalm 119:105

I hope the words in this little collection challenge you to ask how you're navigating, make sure you have solid companions to journey with, and truly know where your compass points.

ONWARD,
　　　R.C. Lloyd

Songs For Your Journey

I Saw The Mountains - Noah Cyrus
Hope - James Bay
Lost & Found - Darren Kiely
Arrow - The Head And The Heart
Run Boy Run - Woodkid
Wolves of Worry - Chance Peña
The Archer - Taylor Swift
Arrows - Trevor Hall
Fought & Lost - Sam Ryder
Treehouse - He Is We
Finish Line - He Is We
Unsteady (Rerecorded) - X Ambassadors
Brother - NEEDTOBREATHE
Way Back Home - Driftwood Choir
Running With You In The Dark - Tenth Avenue North
Stars Are On Your Side - Ross Copperman
Spark of Hope - Davide Wimbish & The Collection
A Little Light - Stars Go Dim
Got It In You - BANNERS
Spirit - Judah & the Lion
Life Won't (It Is Well) - One Common
Love - Alex Serra

PART I:

On Being Lost

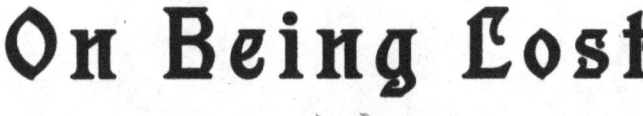

SMALL voices in the leaves whisper lies
Disguised as love notes to your nervous system
Faintly / a breeze / doves cooing
There's wolves biting at your heels
The one in the mirror
Isn't you at all
Your courage comes from within
And when you can't find it / all is lost
For no one else will carry the lantern
And you're the only one who knows
The direction of your heart's compass anyway

Their loudest lie?
If you're lost
You'll surely never be found

AND at your birth
A map was carved in your bones
With each ring / new growth
With new growth / new fears
With new fears / new doubts

And how will you make it out alive
Of this dark body / these dark woods
Your bones have always known the way
But how do you read your bones
Without tearing into your flesh

And perhaps the map on your skin is enough
Intricate / blues / greens / purples
Bruises / blood / coursing under your surface
A living map tracing your veins
Straight to your heart

And will you need bone / blood
To navigate these woods / evade the wolves
To skirt territories of terror
To avoid being drowned
Or is your skin enough

HAVE you noticed how
When the wolves are out / the path is dark
Shadowed by trees obscuring the stars

When you find yourself running
The path grows icy
And your feet slip from under you

When you hear the hawk scream
The trail becomes brambly
And you cannot get anywhere without stumbling

When you climb trees to escape
The way is lined with poison ivy
And snakes greet you from above

When you look for somewhere to hide
The trees are too spindly for cover
And your breathing is the loudest it's ever been

Have you ever tried to stand in the center of the path
To shake your fist at the wood
And plant yourself among the forest unafraid

Have you stood to fight
As you make your claim that you belong here
Same as all the other creatures

For where your fear ends
You stop running and hiding
And from there your path begins to clear

WHEN they said run boy run
You didn't understand how fast

How fast do you run away?
How fast do you turn to what you fear?

How fast do you blame those you love?
How fast do you blame those who love you?

When they said run girl run
You didn't know for how long

How long have you been on the run?
How long since you rested your head?

How long since you trusted?
How long since you were loved?

When they said run child run
You didn't know how hard it would be

How hard it would be to fly
When your wings were clipped

How hard it would be to run
When your heart was weary

What do you wish you'd known
Before they told you to run?

The harder you push your body
The faster you clear your mind
Pushing vines / screeching aside
Clearing the path with a roar
A loudness from within

For when you stand tall
The howling cowers
In its own ring of darkness
Encircling / stalking you
And it is afraid of your body
So you must not be

You must not hesitate
To climb higher than it can leap
Sprint faster than it can run
To dance through the moonlight
Speckled across your path
As you outrun your fears
Cutting off the anxiety

For when you are in your body
Your mind cannot catch you
And what cannot catch you
Cannot devour you

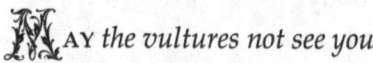

AY the vultures not see you

And when you set off on your journey
Know most of your companions
Will be picked off by birds of prey

May the kites be knocked from the sky

I'm sorry no one told you
Just how fast they fly
Some skim clouds at 240 miles an hour

May the falcons fumble in their pursuit

This is less about the fear / more about the loneliness
For it happens when they least expect it
Until you're the only one left standing

May the hawks fly into brambles

Losing your companions to the birds
Is a burden your heart will never fully set down
Don't let the carrying stop you from the journeying

May the condors be torn to shreds by mountain lions

You should've been warned
That many enter the forest in packs
Yet they leave alone

May the osprey drown before it reaches you

THISTLEHEART HOME

R.C. LLOYD

Have you ever picked apart an owl pellet?
Densely packed with fur that once
Kept a small woodland creature warm
And the bones it once used to run

Imagine these tiny bones in the legs
Propelling a mouse over and under
Logs and stones and hills
Darting between trees in fear
Desperately searching for a hole
One to disappear into

Only to fail
To be captured by the claws
Of a great winged beast
And borne up into the air

Eyes wide
Taking in the entire forest
For the first time
Squeaking a goodbye
For the last time

I'm sorry to be the one to tell you
You can do everything right
And still become an owl pellet

For the hunted don't often
Find their own happy endings

Have you ever had that cold feeling
You know the one

Where eyes bore through your back
Sending chills down your spine
Shooting shivers into your soul

Where your heart sinks
Down in your chest
Forming a pit you know you'll fall into

Where the woods creep closer with every step
Closing in on you
Wrapping darkness around your throat

Or is it just me?
Just me?
Cool. Cool. Cool.

THISTLEHEART HOME

THE cold wants you dead
And so too it seems do the birds of prey
For they've been circling above all night
Pick / pick / picking off your companions
It's only a matter of time before they dive at you

And the wolves have already torn through your flesh
You've been bleeding for so long
Leaving a trail of rubies
As you drag your frame along the once sparkling snow

The crows have aligned to observe your demise
Prepared to empty your pockets
Collect your eyes and fly off
To brag to the cold about their spoils

The cold wants you dead
So it seeps through your bones with every step
Threads ice through your veins
And wraps dread around your lungs
Demanding you to succumb

MAYBE if there were more of you
With lanterns to pierce the darkness

Maybe if you outnumbered the wolves
You could've pierced their flesh

Maybe if your party wasn't so small
The forest couldn't have picked one of you off

Perhaps this is why
You do not enter the wood alone

So many do
And this is how we lose them

Lost souls wandering the wood
Lost souls without an army

Desperately chasing patches of moonlight
Desperately trying to keep the cold at bay

Running / tripping
Falling / freezing

No one to pick them up
Dust them off

No one to hold the lantern
Torch the night

No one to fend the wolves off
From their broken prey

Maybe you had an army
Maybe it didn't make a difference

Maybe there are just battles we win
And battles we lose

Maybe we just have to be okay with that
Lest the darkness swallow us too

How dare the darkness
Have the power to rob you of
Your sleep / your peace / your friend

The darkness took a life
Moments before light broke through
A small way from hope

How dare the darkness
Demand so much
Yet let you pass through

You're harmed / scathed / burned
Sure / but the darkness let you go
And held onto one you were journeying with

Be careful not to let
Almosts / should'ves / could'ves
Swallow you whole in your grief

Because you emerged into the light
Because you were here in the morning
Because he wasn't

Go ahead and rage
Let the anger wash over you
Find comfort in the love persisting as grief

Go ahead and ask your burning question
How dare the darkness
Let you meet the dawn alone

THE mountains convened
Calling on stars / trees
Bodies of water / voices of winds
To congregate for a moment of silence

Sorrow rippled out from the clouds
Gray in memory / tears softly falling
The loons sang a funeral dirge
Whistling the last song on their journey

In this present darkness sometimes all you can do
Is let yourself rage / anger loosing the binds of sadness
Untangling grief wound tightly around your core
Let yourself wail with the coyotes and foxes
Standing on mountaintops together / screaming
At the stars and moon who don't hear
At the God who does

In this present darkness sometimes all you can do
Is let yourself weep when the sun rises
For some days the forest feels too cruel
To deserve the sun's warmth / light
But that's love / unearned / constant

In this present darkness sometimes all you can do
Is fill pockets / flood caverns with your tears
Feeling their weight for a moment
Letting them wash over you / even hold you under
So you won't feel their weight for a lifetime

Sometimes darkness demands more from you
So give it time / rage / tears / but do not
I repeat / do not give yourself into it
Instead lean into resounding grief
But hold fast to peace to lift you out of it

WHEN your tears fall there's a shudder
As the trees grow silent giving you space
To be the restless one
Stretching their arms to the heavens
To praise when you can't
And to cover your head

Perhaps they'll keep their leaves
Just a touch longer this autumn
For you to be the one who lets go
To let what was once new and beautiful
Fall to the ground and die
Isn't that what happens every time anyways?

THISTLEHEART HOME

Your heart is once more learning to be kind to winter
And begging winter to be kind to you

Your heart is determined not to let the cold break you
Brittle shards flying everywhere as battle cries

Your heart is begging to be freed from its cage
Drumbeat pounding as paws on dirt

Your heart is stitching calm into frenzied beats
Building bravery with frostbitten fingers

WHEN grief looks like anger
You turn to the skies
The crows shriek around you
There's wolves at your back

The trees bend in towards you
The branches they fly
Flaming arrows directed
At all who pass by

Your throat contains thunder
Your eyes contain ice
Your jaw set in stone
Your words cut as a knife

When grief looks like anger
Each curve becomes cruel
You choose to attack
To be safe / you are brutal

Is it cruel you went into the wood
Their sacred space
And whittled their initials away

Is it cruel you told the trees
About the ones who hurt you
And the trees cursed them

Is it cruel you asked the forest
To cover paths once taken with thistles
So they'd get lost on their return

For the wood belongs to you now
The trees remember
And the forest chose sides

WALK with your matches held to the trees
Waiting for them to strike / to ignite

Burn the forest as it opens to you / run
Letting the flames chase you down the path

This is fear / fear is weakness
You set fire to the ones you loved

You destroy hopes you once held
You are destruction in a skeleton

Your skin will not be singed
You will walk away unscathed

With your head held high
You will not turn back

You can never return
You are wildfire

For if you walk with your matches held to the trees
Yours is a shadow of ashes / fears / weakness

AND when the wolves hunt you / follow your map home as they lay chase / for if you have something to run towards / you'll be more determined than afraid

When you're being chased / hold your lantern high / run / don't trip on roots / the lantern tip tip tipping / spilling oil all over the wood as it falls / fire flooding the forest / let it burn

If you burn the forest / you burn the wolves / if you burn the wolves / you burn your fears / you go from hunted to hunter / you are safe from all but the smoke / if you burn the forest / you're only left with the ashes

What drove you to run in the first place? When did you first smell the smoke / see the blaze / hear the wolves / feel the fear strike through your heart / realize you were being hunted? Do you know for sure you're being hunted?

When you reach that reflecting pool / watch the fire dance on the lake / see your yellow gleaming eyes / intent / determined / have you considered that perhaps you were the wolf the whole time?

WHY do you bow down in worship
Next to reflecting pools
Arrange your skirts around you
Gaze upon yourself

You tear your skin to pieces
Paint your face with poison
Starve yourself to be seen
Begging to be loved

Somewhere along the darkened path
When chasing perfection
You lost yourself in the woods
And you can't find your way out

Liar became your name
When you traded truth for a mask
To blend in with the royals you feared
The ones you want so desperately to love you

Don't you see the beauty
Staring back from that still water
You are she / she is kind
Kind is beautiful

Why do you bow down in worship
Twisting yourself to an ideal
If your mask ever cracked
Would you know the girl underneath?

"There is no fear in love, but perfect love casts out fear."
1 John 4:18

THERE is no fear in love
So then / cup your fears in your hands
Letting them spill over
As you bring them into the light

What of the terror of being known
Only to be despised or worse
Only to be forgotten perhaps?

What is love if not being known
And what is being known if not a path
One that winds through deep forests
Filled with ghostly songs
Cairns commemorating lost loves
And carvings in trees of the you before me

What is love if not someone to take your hand
And wander deep into forests with you
Holding lanterns to keep your darkness at bay
You are so worth knowing

Let me rephrase
Perfect love casts out fear

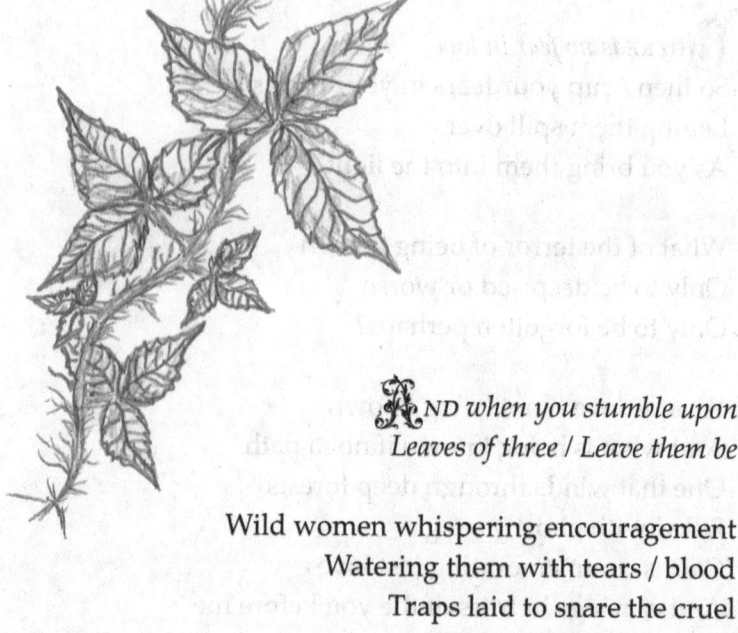

*A*ND *when you stumble upon*
Leaves of three / Leave them be

Wild women whispering encouragement
Watering them with tears / blood
Traps laid to snare the cruel

Tangled hair / pain / strength
Homegrown from cruelty after cruelty
Gardening borne of held rage

Learned from their mothers / who
Learned from their mothers / who
Learned from their mothers / so it goes

Will you be the one who steps off the trail
Cruelties slipping from your tongue?
Or will you join the line of mothers

Daughters who learned
To be women with poison under their nails
Too affected by love / to be affected by the pain

Trust me when I say to fear / respect
The mothers / daughters / grandmothers
Leaves of three / Leave them be

R. C. LLOYD

WHAT is the spine tingling cost
Of being a woman in the woods?
A wife in the forest?
A mother in the trees?

Have you gotten up on your tiptoes
Reached for your femininity
Only to have your hand slapped away
By the whispering wood

Do you reach for more
Only to be held back by your role in this story?
Or do you reach for tradition
Only to find your hopes going up in smoke?

And when you lean into your softness
Do the trees call you weak
While the same ones call you brash
When you stand tall / brave among them

It stings, doesn't it?
To have your ambitions mocked
To have your hopes dashed
To try / try / fail

What if you never become
Wife or mother?
What if you do?
Which terrifies you more?

You foolish human you
You thought crossing the bridge would be free
Or perhaps the toll would be a riddle
Something small trolls mumble under shooting stars

Tell me human / what's across the cascading water?
What dreams embolden you to journey on?
Do you rescue the princess or slay your dragons?
Do you build her a castle / give her a key?

You foolish human you
To cross this bridge you must pay the price
To pay the price you must sacrifice
A drop of blood / a vial of tears

And most importantly
You must face your fears
So tell me human what haunts you?
What makes you curl in terror?

Tell me and I'll bring it out
You gather your blood / tears
I'll gather your fears
And we'll trade

Does that sound fair? No?
Good / that means the toll is appropriate
For to reach your dreams
You must conquer your demons

Down that trail is a maple syrup forest
Where powdered sugar falls from the sky
Brown sugar dusts the path
Gummy worms drop as snakes from the trees
And a river of chocolate calls your name
Swim / drink / dunk / drown yourself in the lava

Oh, did I forget to tell you?
If you go down that path, you'll drown

For down that trail everything can kill you
Temptations glitter as beautiful
Their sweetness rotting at first taste
Their sugary coating corrupting you
When you get down to the bitter truths they cover up

For down that trail is the most beautiful forest
But it's also the most dangerous
The sweetest things always are
You'd think it would be hard to lose yourself
Where you can follow the smell of freshly baked lies

But trust me when I tell you
Following your temptations as trail markers
Will only get you more lost

Do you long for treasure?
Riches beyond reach
Ones nestled deep under mountains
Guarded by dragons

Do you pray for diamonds?
For gifts given to all but you
Do you feel powerless in love
And so hoard what small tastes you get

Do you trust in gold?
To beat back the darkness
To conquer the loneliness
Even precious metals have limits

Do you know your worth?

AND when you chart your path
Know you will encounter dragons
There's no getting around them

Dragons of the east will tear your heart out
Dragons of the west squeeze your heart too tightly
Both will make you bleed

SOMEWHERE along the path
You'll learn that emotional pain
Can physically hurt
That the pain of
All your drownings
Your frigid fingers / bloodied jaw
All battle scars you wear
Are no match to having your heart torn out
And carried away
Clutched in a dragon's claws

THISTLEHEART HOME

I KNOW *you don't believe me when I say*
That you'll make it out alive this time
That you'll survive this / as you always do
Remember your rescues

Remember when the ground split open
When the earth tried to swallow you whole
When you grabbed at a tree root
Only for it to tear away

And send you tumbling into the depths
Of the dragon's den
Into the arms of serpents
Where darkness made a nest for you

Remember how someone threw you a rope
Calling you back into the light
Holding fast as you clawed your way out
Desperation painted as dirt under your fingernails

Remember that first breath of freedom
Panting on the edge / standing above it all
Bloodstains along your hemline and sleeves
Sunshine on your broken skin

CAUGHT you peering down a wishing well
A penny for your thoughts
For the lies that you believe
The ones you tell yourself to sleep at night

A penny / for you're better off alone
Where you can't hurt anyone else
Where your weaknesses can't be someone else's downfall
Where you don't break those you love

A penny / for you're guilty
After all / you're strong enough to carry the blame
After all / you were the reason it happened that way
After all / it's your fault

A penny / for your nightmares
For you'll never escape them
Especially not when they're living / breathing
Stalking you in daylight

A penny / for you're a failure
Always slip slip slipping up
Never quite able to shoulder all the burdens required
Always letting someone down

A penny for / you'll never make it far
You're not strong enough to make it alone
You cannot climb mountains / fight dragons
It's all simply too hard

A penny for / your dreams are too big for this world
After all / not everyone gets their happy ending
And why would you be so lucky
Why would you be the exception?

Let me gather up your pennies / whisper a prayer
Toss them in the wishing well
Cast your lies below / leave them all behind
Replace them with the truth ahead
After all / they were only lies anyways

WHAT if getting lost was a price?
You let your heart be pixie-led
And listened to the fairies whisper
You chose not to plug your ears
And danced to their words instead
For their voices were sweet
Promising / pretty
Eyes wide / fluttering
Trusting you just enough
For you to trust them

What if getting held captive was a price?
You held out your wrists
So they could braid ivy around them
Decorating you / your life
With joy / beauty / woodland creatures
With soft meadows / bright flowers
Delicate fairy jewelry holding your hands
In captivity
Your fate bound to theirs

How do you escape the fae?
Can you ever outpace them?
These woods are in their bones
They mapped trails to open / close
To their voices alone

How do you untangle your heart from one so cruel?
Perhaps by taking one small step at a time
One small no at a time
One small defiance

Perhaps by trusting one small confidence
To friends who would untie your binds
To family who would burn the wood to protect you

THISTLEHEART HOME

On discerning kind dryads from cruel ones
When they take your hand to dance
You must notice / notice / notice

Notice the lightness with which they
Pull you in to dance amidst howling winds
Pushing away your fears with springtime air

Notice their roots rippling through the dirt
Wrapping around your ankles
Forcing you to keep in step with them

Notice their gentle but firm touch
Lacing your shoes up your delicate calves
Waking a light flutter in your chest

Notice the thorns stitching your lips shut
Until you cannot speak up for yourself
After all / the trees don't always want to hear you

Notice the freedom they give you
To follow the stars / as they follow your eyes
Steadying you as you dream

Notice the moths erupting from their mouth
Filling your mind with buzzing lies
Turning you into what you fear

Notice the cherry blossom truths twirling
Guiding you on with their song / scented wildwood
Marriage of strength and softness freeing you

Notice how with your partner
You're light on your feet / left flushed with joy
Or constantly at a loss / left bleeding out

DID you know hunters
Track deer
Wait with their bow
Aimed at the heart

I'm sorry you thought
They were journeying with you
I'm sorry that
Their attention felt like love

As the cold sets in
They grow hungry
They loose their arrow
And carry your bloodied carcass home on their shoulders

Run before your hunter breaks your heart
Before they turn you into their next meal
Follow the deer paths home
Now you're free

When you run
You'll make it
Leaps and bounds further
Than you could by their side

THISTLEHEART HOME

AND if you're still running
When this reaches you

Meet me in the fossilized forest
Wander the remnants of the Holocene

Where ash / fire once rained down
Burying us in sentiment / sediment

Where the lifeblood of trees drained
Where minerals bled into the wood

Where saltwater tears crystallized
As we cried ourselves to sleep

Are you petrified?
It's okay, I am too

It's just quartzite growing in the wood
As pain turns to memory in your chest

THE forest swallowed you
This you know for sure
But somehow you swallowed the forest too

Somewhere between being chased by wolves
Ducking under treetops
Hiding from screeching birds of prey
And praying to your God that you would be spared

Perhaps it happened when you stumbled
Skinning your knee
Giving the wolves an opportunity to pounce
As you cleaned gravel and dirt from the wound
Wrapped bandages around it
Hobbled through the darkness
On the night starlight
Was denied entry to the wood

Yes / it was somewhere in there
That you swallowed the forest
You know because you can feel it in your chest
Tangled roots winding
Around your stomach / lungs / heart
Protruding from your throat
Choking you

Yes / that's right
You may be lost in the wood
But you should be more concerned
With the trees growing in your chest
Taking over your organs
Soon you'll be more forest than flesh

WHEN you say you're lost
Do you mean you don't know your way around
This being you inhabit
That they are wild
More beast than man
That the heart called yours sometimes refuses
To fall into step with your rhythms
That your chest sometimes tightens at
Unrecognizable faces in mirrors
That you know the patterns of stars
Better than the back of your own hand
That the light doesn't always reach
This deep into the forest
So you have to rely on memories to navigate
Those untamed wolves you keep as pets
Fangs bared / waiting for you to show weakness

When you say you're lost
Do you mean that your nightmares are often
More familiar than your dreams

WHEN fog lays thick
And briars gnaw at your ankles

When moon curls in blankets of clouds
And darkness covers the wood

When stars cease shining
And you've forgotten the taste of light

When wolves and wind
Howl in perfect harmony

Do you lay your cape in shadows
And cower on the forest floor?

Do you give up / give in
And let the moss envelope you?

Is this when you finally rest
Or do you strike a flame from your heart?

And hold a bloodied lantern high
To keep the darkness at bay?

And now I lay me down to sleep
I pray the Lord my soul to keep

ALL the wolves you kept as pets
Came out to play in dreams

To taunt and rob you of your sleep
To rob you of your peace

The dangerous creatures you once housed
The ones you fed / loved

The ones that tore your skin to shreds
The ones that ripped your heart

The ones that drowned you in the brook
The ones that held you under

The ones you fear / the ones you hurt
The ones who tried to love

The ones that made you hate yourself
The ones you'd go back to

The ones you wish you'd never met
The ones that led you here

Perhaps they came to play in dreams
Simply to say goodbye

Perhaps to lay themselves to rest
Before they're left behind

THISTLEHEART HOME

And when you're laying there on the forest floor
Slipping your way between dream / reality / dream
Forest / sky / treetops / clouds / moonbeam
The huntsman gently scoops up your broken frame
And suddenly you're whole again
Entering the wood unbroken
Healed / hand in hand / a child
Innocence / love as stars in your eyes

Or are those mine?
This is my journey
So I can tell you
It won't last / it never does
Don't hold on too tightly

INTERLUDE:

The Wicked Woods

THERE once was a girl on the run
Let's call her Little Red
Winter in her bones / heart of shattered ice
She was timid / evercold / determined
Not to let fragility define her story

There once was a boy who bled life
Into everything he touched
Let's call him *her* Huntsman
Summer in his blood / heart of a champion
He was brave / relentless in his pursuit of joy
Yet patient enough to tug her along

Our story begins as two step foot down the garden path
Hand in hand / they did that much right
He her compass / her his heart
Together they knew the way
Woolen mittens clasped together / keeping the cold at bay

With each dawn they journeyed on
Wild children in a wilder wood
Clinging to each other / clinging to the known
Clinging to the love that comes from being known
Clinging to the light that comes from the love
Journeying down paths / illuminated from their light

ᏝET's blow out the candle
So we can see our small shadowy figures
Silhouettes against the dim morning sky
Ambling down the path
Making progress past bushes smacking them in the face
Ducking for cover as the bats
And birds of prey dive at them
Boldly pressing on / until they reach a coursing river

The huntsman crosses first
Making bridges of stones and logs
Making a way / telling Little Red to follow
Urging her on
Her toes touch the first rock and slip into frigid waters
Everpresent / eversteady
Her huntsman catches her hand
Pulls her along / tugs her to the other side
She doesn't slip again

See the darkness set in / see them set up camp
See their haven from the frost
He sets her riverdrenched boots
To dry on stones by the fire
She heats stew to warm their bones / fill their stomachs
They eat in silence under starlight / by firelight
Kept company by the crackling of fire
The howling of wolves

Under darkness / they grow closer
Make each other braver
On cold nights / they make fires
Share stories of warmer days
Ones where the woods are kind
Where the boy and girl are brave
And where the moonlight is bright
Enough to illuminate the forest
For the only fear they know is the dark / after all
It's all they've faced

See Little Red and her Huntsman
Sprawled out on forest floor by firelight
Sticks tracing the dirt / designing their castle / future
They'll make it out of the woods
To the place they'll call home
Together they'll build a palace of light
They truly believed that anyways

It's important for you to know
These woods were home to wolves
Packs and loners / fears and lies
Poised to tear our little heroes apart
For the wood is cruel
Snuffs out every flame of hope it can
It demands / and demands
And demands every ounce of courage
Till there's none left

When the wolves first come to call
Our little ones face them down
She tames some with her kindness
He fights those she could not reach
For wolves are terrors / some fears need a gentle touch
Some just need love
Still others turn to cruelty
That can only be carved out of hearts

For this reason our heroine counts herself lucky
Her Huntsman carries courage
In the same hand as his knife
Together they stand against the wolves
Brave enough to love the hurting
Brave enough to do the hard thing
Together they journey on
Protecting the creatures of the forest from the wolves
Protecting the woods from darkness
With every fire they light

WATCH our heroes grow older
Watch the forest grow with them
Watch them pour courage and kindness from their hands
Watch the forest return it with favor
Gather round to celebrate them
Braiding crowns of flowers / roots winding into thrones
Willows bowing as our tiny royalty
Ascends to claim their thrones

Our Huntsman King / Our Little Red Queen
Royalty / eternal / unstoppable
Together / small brave immortals
Crossing many galaxies hand in hand
Taming and carving many wolves
Lighting fires / warming woods
Chasing wisps down garden paths
Leading one another / leading the forest well

R.C. LLOYD

AFTER rivers and mountains and valleys
One cruel Autumn day
The leaves begin to fall
Mourning a loss they don't know
Their time is ending / as all times are bound to do
A reign of brevity / eternity / the lifespan of a firefly
Watch their light blink / blink / blinking out
Poor Little Red / unprepared to relinquish her throne
Poor Little Red / so afraid to be alone

Listen closely / perhaps you can hear the song of the sea
The sirens calling / the whales whispering in his heart
The very ones that called him away
Watch closely / perhaps you can see him tilt his head
First he listens / then he leaves
Perhaps you'll even see him go

Watch even closer and you'll see him leave her
Sleeping soundly / believing she's safe
Under her cape / under the stars
Blissfully unaware / mere hours away from breaking

AND when she wakes in dead of night / her
Huntsman's slipped away
The wood became a wicked place
The stars refused to shine
Their fire that night chose not to light
The sun chose not to rise
The starlit night turned inky black
Darkness swallowed her whole

She didn't see it coming / how could she ever have
Why would he wander off from hope
Why would he let go of the only warmth he'd ever known
Why would he leave his heart behind
In bloodthirsty woods that prey on ones who trek alone

Together they were separated / separate lost their way
On that starless night / our Little Red was lost
No compass / no hand to hold
She runs through the wood unmoored
Bravely she steels herself to face malevolence alone

SEE the fear painted on her face / her mask made of ice
The first time the wolves come to call
And he's not by her side
For wolves can smell fear
And the wood knows her weaknesses
It's been stalking her since she entered / biding time
She turns to try to tame the wolves
To find a home in them
For she used to walk among the fears
She used to heal their hurt

But oh her surprise when she learns
They'll readily hurt her too
All the wolves see her as prey now that she's all alone
For her Huntsman shielded her
From so much more than she knew
When her wolves grew cruel / left him with no choice
He'd carve them up / carry her away / wipe her tears

Alone she tries and tries most desperately
To save one of their hearts / to foster a new companion
To find someone so she won't have to walk on alone
But wolves have claws / their howls bare teeth
They tear her heart to shreds / her bones turn cold

Alone and hurting on the forest floor
Little Red has lost all hope
This is the darkest point in her story
Where she wants to give up

To not light the fire / to unbutton her cloak
To succumb to the cold
For it promises quiet / safety / wrapped in nothingness
And nothingness would surely be better
Than missing her Hunter
In fact / anything would be better

SMELL the petrichor as the forest cries with Little Red
Listen closely and perhaps you can hear her sobs
Her family hears her too / see them come running
See them lift her up / dust her off / bandage her wounds
See their love shine through their actions

She'll let them in / let them carry her for a time
This is an act of courage
For it takes courage to show weakness
This is an act of love / for they love her dearly

She'll take the help
For picking up the shattered pieces of her life is hard
Each piece is sharp / a memory slicing though her hands
Bloodying her fingers
Bleeding out on the pure white snow

She'll let them piece her broken heart together
Stitching it with strength
Reminders that she will love again
But for now she is loved / and that is enough

Watch as they arm her/ with scripture / prayers / love
A sword / a shield / a lantern / a horn to call for help
Lifting / lacing / buckling her armor on her thin frame
Packing supplies for her journey ahead
For she still has far to go
But this time / she's not alone

Look / our little heroine
Standing side by side with her loved ones
Holding her very own lantern high
Brandishing light against the inky sky
Dutifully plodding through snow
For she must journey on

She still has fears to grapple with
Doubts to face
Anger to come to terms with
She's armed / no longer alone
But still / she must face things

Will she blame the wicked wood for tearing them apart?
Will she blame her Woodsman for leaving her behind?
Or will she blame her bleeding heart
For letting herself love
For by opening up her heart to love / she opened it to loss

For nights she wrestles
Finding love buried in the grief
Finding good in the love to hold on to
Finding she can let go even if it was good
Finding she can move on on as she lets go

SEE Little Red find freedom in moving forward
See her let others back into her life
Watch our queen build her castle
Hand in hand with the small army that heard her cry

Together repairing her broken heart
From disarray to beauty
Painting her own stained glass with clouds
And hanging her wilted flower crown to dry
Next to two woolen mittens / strung up on her hearth

And on nights when when the cold comes to call
When wolves howl outside her gates
When stars refuse to shine
Little Red turns to see companions by her side
She finds them keeping the hearth stoked
Keeping her warm

She finds herself dearly hoping / sending up a prayer
That the Huntsman King has friends by his side too
That he is safe / warm somewhere
No longer hers / forever loved

112.

PART II:

On Being Found

AND when you slip from dream
My words paint wariness at the edges of your mind
And all at once you wonder
Is it better to enter the woods alone
Or to be abandoned along your way
A warm hand slipping from your cold one
A grief flooding your bleeding heart
A loss so profound it shapes your path
Two woolen mittens all that's left
Of a future you were running towards

This is my journey
So I can tell you
The story doesn't end there

DID you lose your compass?
Was your heart shaken so much
By the drowning / dreaming / darkness
That it no longer points North
That you no longer know where to go

Did your heart break?
When you went your separate ways
When you realized you were alone
You must chart your own path now
He never was true North

Did the woods change to reflect your heart?
When you fled to the shadows
Dark / cold / all alone
Your path twisting in fear
Your eyes overcome by rain

Did you find your way?
When you saw the light
When you were called out of darkness
For no one can separate you
From the love / light / truth

Did you let them in?
When your companions heard your cries
When they looped their arms through yours
And tugged you forward
Into the light

Will you follow the light?
Or succumb to the darkness
You know the way out
Requires faith / courage
You've had both all along

OH dreamer
It's time for the waking
Oh lift up your eyes
To the hills
To the sun
To the stars

Oh dreamer
It's time for the walking
Ready yourself for the journey
To find yourself
Your home
Your people

Oh dreamer
It's time for the darkness
Take up the armor
The shield
The sword
The light

Oh dreamer
It's time for the fighting
Stand firm
Level your sword
Loose your arrows

OH dreamer
It's time for the mourning
For every war comes with losses
Take a moment of silence
For the one the darkness robbed us of

THISTLEHEART HOME

OH dreamer
It's time for the victory
For you forged ahead bravely
And now you get to live
For beauty
For love
For light

Oh dreamer
It's time for the dancing
Hold your loved ones closer and spin
Into the night
Into the stars
Far beyond the sunrise

THISTLEHEART HOME

WHEN you wake
I hope you find yourself in someone's arms
Held close / perhaps even prayed over

For the forest is a little bit warmer where you are held
A little bit brighter with sparkling eyes
To illuminate the darkness
A little more hopeful when you are loved

THE bravest souls are forged of fireflies
Funeral dirges / absolute devastation

Did you know music comes from light
Floating through the trees
Did you know light comes from kindness
The truest of hearts
Did you know kindness comes from safety
Rooted in candor
Did you know safety comes from knowing
What do you know?

Do you know what danger feels like
Do you know what it feels like to be stalked as prey
Do you know what it feels like
To be hunted as you run in terror
Do you know what it feels like
To be seen but never understood

Have you yet faced the darkness
With a song in your heart
Have you yet taken stones
And engraved kindness in your bones
Have you yet stitched your true heart
Back together from cruelties
Have you yet returned to the wood
To guide other souls through

The bravest souls sing against silence
Follow fireflies home / leave trails for others to follow

DEEP in the murky wood
Is an ocean of fears
Under scatters of starlight
That filter through treetops
Piercing deep waters
Beams of starlight to guide you
Through deep seas
Navigate deep space
And finally find your place
At the edge of the woods

When you go through deep waters
I am with you

"When you pass through the waters, I will be with you; and through the rivers, they shall not overwhelm you; when you walk through fire you shall not be burned, and the flame shall not consume you."

Isaiah 43:2

AND under the stars
All at once your mother's prayers return to you
For Heavenly protection
For courage / candor / compassion

These are your woods
And if you are good to them
They'll guide you home

The moon will illuminate your path
And Guardians of the forest
Will watch over you

Your mother's prayers reached the stars
And Heaven responded
Commanding Guardians concerning your mortal frame

LEGEND has it that
You're never alone

No matter how deep
Into the wildwood
Your heart wanders
From your bones

Moss Angels
With hearts of light
Guardians of stone
Brave the night

They stand among the trees
Cradling sunlight
A waterfall spilling over
Their arms to light your path

They part the crowns of trees
And let the glow reach the dirt
Warming your bones
Guiding you home

Follow footprints in the snow
Revealing those who went before

Heavy boots for heavy hearts
Carrying loads of tragedy / fear

But still they walked on
Seeking a home / like you

Your ancestors / mentors / mothers
Fathers / grandfathers / grandmothers

All the greats / all were lost once
You are lost / but you will be found

Take wisdom from their lessons
See the paths they took

Let the ways carved be your guide
And follow their footprints left behind

At a fork in the path something inside you splits
As you realize you can no longer
Remain who you once were

That fearful / terrorized child
The one running scared
The one with words careless as daggers

Not if you want to grow anyway
For you cannot be the child you once were
And the adult you are becoming

You cannot be brave and cower in fear
Cannot hold hope in the same hand as despair
Cannot be brutal and kind

This is a turning point
Will you follow the light leading to truth
Dappled along the path / calling you higher

Or will you venture deeper into the forest
Where the woods whisper your name
And darkness offers a cruel familiarity

And I pray that you find
Yourself in that space
Between predator and prey

For to survive the forest
So many get pushed into roles
Play the wolf or the rabbit

What is your role in this story?
Cast off where you've been cast
To find your way home

For to read the map
Is to know yourself
Is to reject your part

If the woods are cruel
And they cast you in a role
Don't play into their claws

For I pray that you are
Neither the hunter
Nor the hunted

May you be a third thing
One that you choose for yourself
May you have courage / be kind

WHEN you see the ring of mushrooms
Tiny / capped / colorful creatures
Tread lightly / for you've stumbled upon a twist

Such curiosities appear occasionally in life
All that's led you here has been preparing you
All that comes after hinges on what you do

Resist the urge to match fairy deceits with yours
Instead unearth the truth in that chest
You've been dragging around

The one you packed carefully as you grew
Those contents chosen from moments
That shaped you and the path you forged

For fae may be cruel
Twisted creatures / twisting lies with truths
But it's your turn / not theirs

Will you act from hate or love?
Will you be honest or lie?
Will you fall or fly?

Step into the ring of mushrooms
Greet the small red creatures
And tell the truth in your heart

LET truth be your compass
Trust your feet know the way
Listen for the cry to arms
Listen for the call home

For you know His voice
As quiet as it may be
As dim as the light is
As faint as the truth may feel

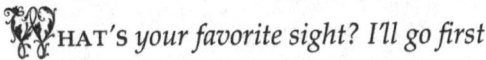 *HAT'S your favorite sight? I'll go first*

You know the feeling when you're alone / you've been wandering through the dark wood all night / without any firelight / for your lantern blinked out hours ago / the cold has seeped through your many coats / you lost your mittens somewhere back there / your stomach is equal parts knotted with fear and crying with hunger / and you've nearly lost hope / not quite / but nearly

Now imagine you see the warm glow of a cabin / a firelight / a lantern / or even a torch / some warm light inviting you home / silhouettes of those who love you / waiting to welcome you / the softest of reminders your hope was grounded in truth / you were right / the glow is a promise / you will be warm / full / loved

That right there / that's my favorite sight to behold

BROTHERS are the fabric of the forest
Bear cubs stumbling / finding their footing
Knit tightly to one another
Tied together with knots learned
From your father
The same one who taught them / you
To climb mountains by
Pulling each other up
Paws laced into a step for the young
Love / pride flowing from the old
No bear left untended
No brother left behind

Over the river and through the woods
  To grandmother's house we go

Where split wood warms the hearth
The hearth warms the kernels of truth
Shared around the flickering flame
Safe in the warm glow of love
The kernels pop / food for thought
Chewing on small kindnesses
Puzzles / presents into the night
Just your presence would be alright
All we ask is you stay
Where you're safe you're warm
Where you're warm you're loved
Go where you're loved

Over the river and through the woods
  To grandmother's house we go

ALL roads lead home means nothing
When you wake in the woods
Thorns embedded in every organ
Broken / bleeding out on the trampled dirt
Dragging your bloodied frame down
Seemingly aimless winding paths
Leading you through the darkest parts
Of your story

But all roads lead to the after
For no matter how lost you feel now
You will find yourself again
You will begin to believe in yourself
Your confidence will grow
And there will be an after

It may not be a happily ever after
It may not be happy for a long time
But you will begin to breathe again
Those vines that wound around your lungs
Can be pulled out with care
Untangled slowly / letting you breathe

Your skinned knees will carry you forward
Your broken bones will mend themselves
Your bleeding heart will reach hemostasis
And you will be okay

R.C. LLOYD

Do you hear me?
You will survive this
You will breathe again
You will be okay

All roads lead home means everything
When you realize that no matter how dark
How bloody / how broken / how far gone
Your frame will heal

I SEE the apathy crawling around your heart / that viney invasive species / whispering promises that it will be a hedge of protection / lies that you won't feel the pain once it's fully covered your body

I know you have fought / I know you have lost / I know you are angry / I know you are trying to thaw the anger / but you've not yet come to the acceptance / and it feels like your only other option is apathy / it is not

Let me repeat myself / apathy is not an option / look to the stars / see just how deep they go / look to the creatures / see how they carry on / look to those around you / see how they care for you / see how deeply they care

I know it feels cruel / to tear yourself away from the one thing that eases the agony / but tear out the damned invasive species / it is human to feel / so feel every hook / barb / root / let it draw blood / let the pain draw blood

Walk the forest with your heart raw / no hedge of false protection / for only when you experience pain fully / deeply in your chest / letting it resound as screams / sobs / gentle tears sheltered by the canopy of those who care deeply for you / only then will you be healed

AND when you go cliff diving
How far will you fall
How high are those falls?

Will your bravery turn to fear
As your legs turn to jelly
Will you do it anyway?

Will your dreams be dashed
On the rocks below
Will your heart be dashed too?

Will you lose your sense of adventure
Of optimism / of hope?
Don't let the falls dash your hopes

No matter how helpless you feel
As the water floods your lungs
As you choke / sputter / claw for the surface

You do not drown here
You will emerge on the other side of the bank
And your lungs will be filled

Take the outstretched hands
Grab the lifelines thrown
Hang on for dear life

R.C. LLOYD

Let your loved ones pull you to shore
Don't fight them / don't pull them down with you
Don't let them drown

Hear me when I tell you this
You do not drown here
You do not drown

Your companions played tug a war
With the darkness while you slept
The forest slowly lost its grip on you
As friends held fast to you

They pulled out thorns
Patched up wounds / stitched up losses
And they were there
Holding your hand when you woke

Your companions fought and won
Untangling the forest's hold on you
On your lungs / for you can draw a deep breath
On your heart / for it beats fiercely once more

FOLLOW me / quickly now
Into the armory
Before you journey on

Load your arms with gold / silver / bronze
Slip these knives in your boots
String that bow over your shoulder

Let your companions heft your breastplate
Strapping it to your chest / protecting your heart
One bends down to lace up your boots
Another hands you a sword

Take up faith as a weapon / hope to light your way
Love to protect against all the lies
For the woods first language is deceit

After all / the woods are out to kill you
And spirits stalk your soul
Waiting on a lapse / for you can't always be strong

At least that's what the trees murmur
As they keep watch / rustling above you
Blocking starlight / keeping you in the dark

In the dark it's easier to make you stumble
If they can get you to stumble / they can get you to fall
Don't let one another fall

Don't journey on alone / for that's how we lost one
Instead buckle your companions armor
And prepare for battle together / as one

"Therefore take up the whole armor of God,
that you may be able to withstand in the evil day,
and having done all, to stand firm."

Ephesians 6:13

May your arrows be dipped in courage
Nocked with certainty

May you advance with your shield up
Throwing caution to the wind is for fools

May you know that retreating is strength
Learned from all the times you didn't

WHEN you fight / don't come out swinging
Light a lantern first
I know you tend to reach for your sharpest edges
And put up your defenses every chance you get

I see how you treasure that sword
Tracing the hilt in times of fear
Rubbing your thumb along the embedded jewels
A comfortable habit to keep fear at bay

I know you've buried your heart somewhere deep
Reinforced by armor / stone walls / leather
The toughest materials you've found in the wood
Pushing everyone away

For if they never get close enough
Then you won't have to fight them
But sometimes your armor slips
And your someone finds a chink

In those moments / don't come out swinging
Light a lantern first
Find the truth / for your fight is not with men
But with the father of lies

The wolves / birds / dragons all do his bidding
Creatures of the night turn to their master
But your master is love / truth / light
You are light

Reach deep inside
Where you have truth engraved in bone
Where you have unspilled blood white as snow
Where you have light nestled in your soul

Light casts out darkness
Love casts out fear
And you were not made with a spirit of fear
But with a spirit of love

THISTLEHEART HOME

My darling let them in
Those who stand at your crumbling stone walls

I know you've become addicted
to the loneliness that dwells within you

I know you're afraid
They'll leave like everyone before did

I know you've been hurt
And refuse to suffer the same fate again

I know you dread
The day you lose someone else again

But your mossy home alone cannot sustain you
And your leather bound armor only isolates you

You may believe you're pushing them out
Holding the line so no arrow pierces your heart

But truth be told,
You're keeping the monsters in

Cease calling them friend, for they are
A deadly sickness you lack the army to face

Drop your guard my darling,
Lest you die alone

WHAT if someone else knows how
To read the map you were given?
Isn't that reason enough
Not to go through life alone?
Even if it means humbling yourself
Enough to hand it over?

In the compromise
Is the art of an ecosystem

As sunlight dappling through treetops
As shadows dancing along the paths
Show them the way
In the way darkness / light

Coexist

How then can wolves / deer
How then can the hunter / hunted
How can the predator / prey
Pray for warmth
Run with deer
Cruelty / kindness
The wood is home to all

But bear in mind

If you live as prey
You will be torn into
For no one is safe
Predators do not compromise
In an ecosystem like ours
It is survival of the strong

The art of an ecosystem
Is the lack of compromise

R . C . LLOYD

(Read in reverse)

THISTLEHEART HOME

CHOOSE your friends carefully
Please / I beg of you
Choose ones who carry you
And choose ones
You find joy in carrying

Hand in hand / arms looped
Pulling one another forward
Catching each other when fall
Taking turns with the burdens
Those packs are lighter when shared

Gathering firewood in the darkness
Is easier with someone by your side
And you are braver
With soldiers at your back
So walk on / in lockstep

And friends / bear in mind
If one keeps the lantern burning
All of you have light to travel by
Bind wounds / light fires / keep warm
And fight for each other

Have you sat around a fire
Sharpening your weapons

Next to your loved ones
Sharing stories of times

Someone threw a rope
Lit a fire / welcomed you in

Someone swooped in to save you
Riding on the back of bravery

Someone stayed up all night with you
To beat back the darkness

Someone wrapped you in prayers
An unseen halo of protection

Your Guardian Angels covered you
Under soft mossy arms

Light a fire / gather round
Share the tales

For you've been saved once
It will surely happen again

I hope you begin to see the woods
As a place of wonder and whimsy
Streaming through the trees
Of love and light and sunshine
Warming you as you journey
Along this winding path

I hope you don't get winded
As you climb mountains
The air gets thinner as you go
But I hope you have friends
Who push you on towards the peak
For the view is glorious

I hope you make it for the sunrise
From my favorite spot on the cliff
Let your feet dangle over the edge
As you lean back on your roots
As the morning light washes over you
Warming your bones

I hope your bones carry you
Safely down the mountain to the pool
For at the bottom is a lake
A looking glass for your soul
Showing you how far you've come
Rippling out to where you have to go

I hope you know you have further to go
Bridges over rushing water to cross
Wishes in wells to make
Creatures to befriend
Dragons to ride / yes / you have yet to fly
You'll fly over the most beautiful meadow

And when you come to the meadow
I hope you wander through wildflowers
Picking your favorites and braiding yourself a crown
Letting your fingers brush the flower petals
Brushing hands with those you love
And closing around them

I hope you keep hiking on
Hand in hand with those you love

WHEN you carry hope
Engraved on your heart
And begin to see the woods
As a place of freedom
An expanse to explore
Rather than a cage
Filled with creatures out for blood

That's when you'll learn to fly
Leaping from the trees
Wings catching the air
Bearing you upwards
Rising with the wind
Flying with the eagles

"But they who wait for the Lord shall renew their strength; they shall mount up with wings like eagles; they shall run and not be weary; they shall walk and not faint."

Isaiah 40:31

On hope / warmth / little woodland creatures
A fluffle of bunnies burrowing
In cushions of glistening snow
Finding warmth together in emboldened cold

On days when the cold is brave
May you be braver

And when you say you're on your way
Do you mean the forest can't contain you?

Do you mean you will find your way home
Because your feet know the way?

Do you mean that soon enough your heart will be held
Your hands warmed / your stomach filled?

Do you mean you're no longer alone
For you found your fastest friends in the forest?

Do you mean this wandering and winter
Will not last / do you mean it never does?

Do you mean that the cold is temporary
And your home is eternal?

"Flowers return to the earth - a time of singing has come."

Song of Solomon 2:12

PERHAPS the sunshine is beginning to thaw the snow
The snow is melting into the groundwater
The groundwater is running into the streams
The streams are rushing down the mountains
The mountains are shouting in the language of waterfalls
The waterfalls are splashing you / one you love

Look, you / one you love are standing hand in hand
Hands holding fast in the pool at the bottom
The pool is cold and numbs your bare toes
Your bare toes are running through meadows
Over the soft grass
The soft grass is giving way to spring blooms
The spring blooms are filling the air with sweet scents
The sweetness of spring invites
Butterflies and bees to join you

Perhaps the sunshine is beginning
To thaw your cold hearts
The crows and daggers are melting
To meadows and gardens

SOMEWHERE it's not you / them
In some far off wood it's both as one
That's where your mind wanders
Walking through green soft meadows
Hand in hand / keeping in step
Marigolds / daisies in bloom
You're sitting on a blanket braiding crowns
Because in your wood you have a meadow
The stone foundation of your greenhouse
Is laid / waiting for the glass to arrive
Butterflies circle you as halos
Because you welcomed them with milkweed
For your meadow in the wood is a home
For bunnies / bugs / both of you together

WHEN you dream of building your castle
Of securing your place in the forest
Is it a monstrous task / Herculean even?

When you think of carrying heavy stones
Carving wooden frames
Soldering stained glass images of battles
Penning books of your victories alone
Are you overwhelmed?

Is it discouraging to know there are
Moments to pen you can't word
Stones to lift you can't carry
Things to fashion you don't have the skills for
You never will

Tell me dreamer
Do you have a scribe to pen your legacy?
A bricklayer to lay your bricks?
A mason for your stone work?
A glass blower for your painted windows?
A carpenter for your door frames?
A seamstress for the drapes
All things soft and welcoming?

Assembling your crew takes bravery
Opening yourself up / letting them in
Building together creates community
Fosters connection / reveals brokenness
Are you ready to reveal your brokenness?

THISTLEHEART HOME

GOD knew you were lonely / so He recruited an army
Friends to take up a sword / ride into battle by your side

To the spontaneous ones / He assigned your spirit
Dancing into the night / losing yourself in the thrill of it

To the patient ones / He assigned your heart
Broken / weary / learning contentment
The definition of insanity

To the soft ones / He assigned your femininity
Flower crowns / friendship bracelets
Have courage / be kind

To the strong ones / He assigned your actions
Foolish in love / fearful in life / reckless in the moment

To the brave ones / He assigned your nightmares
Wild / clawing / dragging insecurities into the daylight

To the quick ones / He assigned your words
Angry / bitter / jaded with heartbreak

To the wise ones / He assigned your soul
How to spend a life / how to leave a legacy
How to be a friend

So gather your army round / thank them for their service
Mount your horses / sound your horn / you ride at dawn

How will you know when it's safe?

When the morning dew
Begins to glisten from more than moonlight
And the sky floods with a glimmer
Midnight blue softening to gentle purple
And the hushed council of owls quiets
Giving way to the chorus of dawn

That's when you'll know you've survived the night

THISTLEHEART HOME

THE sun will rise / light peeking through trees
Illuminating the friends riding by your side

You set out into the darkness alone
But you have since gained brothers / sisters
Seated on wild stallions / your hearts are wild

The sun will rise / light peeking through the trees
Glinting off the armor you all wear

A soundtrack of swords thumping against saddles
Hoofs thumping against ground
War cries going ahead / fear left behind

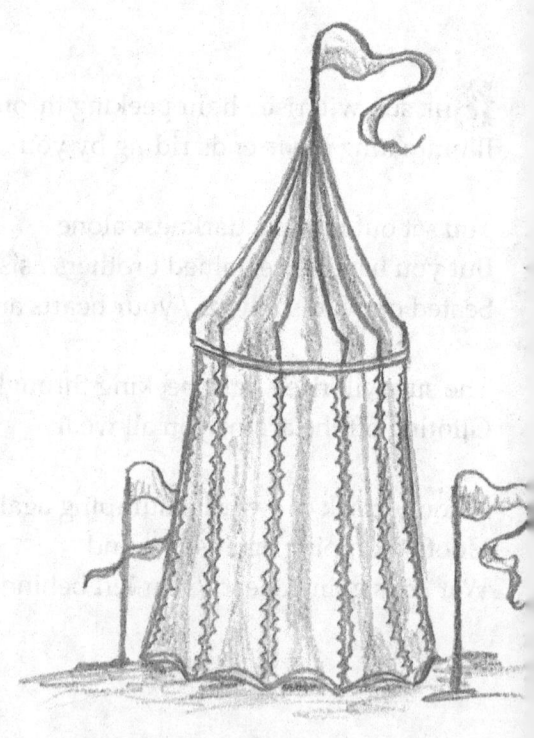

SOUND your horn / resounding across the wood
Calling your companions and confidants
To come for tea / for strategy
Gather your troops here in the meadow

For nature adorned your picnic
Hanging golden dewdrops from the weeping willow
Arranging flowers around your chosen spot
And draping sunlight across the blankets

These bright tents with bunting dancing in the wind
Conceal tables of maps and models
Wars mapped / played / already won
For when you gather / you've already won

Pour the sweetest wines and let them overflow
Cheering from golden goblets
Let your songs loose to the heavens
Tell the stars of your victory

GATHER round kings / queens of this land
Usher in the Golden Age
For your heads were crowned
Beloved / a title no one can take away
Flood the deserted castle with life
Rise from rubble to fortress

One for lost travelers to stumble on
Over years / under starlight
When they're sprinting hunted
Through the tangled wood
Clutching their dagger to cut through
Brambles reaching for their ankles

And in the armory leave your worn armor as gifts
For they've served you well
In the journey / in the battles / in the war
They've seen you through darkness
And brought you into light
Now may they serve souls who come after you

And when the years turn to centuries
When the forest is full of creatures
Whose ancestors hunted or protected you
When this tangled wood turns to an old growth forest
When your castle becomes ruins
May those ruins always welcome weary travelers

May your reign protect souls for centuries
Long may you reign

ACKNOWLEDGMENTS

ThistleHeart Home is the first project I've found a home
in. I hope you found one too. But homes aren't built in
isolation; they're built with many hands and much love.
Because of this, I have many to thank.

Nathaniel, you invited me to publish with Dragon Heart
Press, witnessed the spark of the idea, helped cultivate it
to a collection, and even contributed to the title. Thank
you for being my fiercest hypeman and loudest advocate.
Publishing with you is a joy.

Effie, you brought my vision to life in such a vivid way. I
am in love with the cover, art, and map. Thank you for
illustrating the tiny creatures and emotions from my
mind.

MJ, you hyped me up, helped me name the collection, and
most importantly, formatted it. How you imbued the
formatting with such creativity and beauty, I'll never
know. Thank you!

My Beta Readers: Sam, Sara, Erin, Nathaniel, you all took
such time and care in reading the collection and sharing
your thoughts. You helped me with everything from
word choice to structure. And your reactions gave me
life. Thank you for joining me in this little home in the
forest.

Jenni, the little group chat with you and Nathaniel is a
small home in and of itself. Thank you for all the ways
you've encouraged me and believed in me, there and in
all things.

All my friends, but especially Josh, Lydia, Karyn, Rain,
Sally, Allie, Jenna, Faith, Abby, Angelina, and Becca, I
love adventuring with you. You make the forest so much
brighter.

And also, Kayla, thanks for listening to the BecaLore. ;D

All the moms who've been by my side, especially this
year; my momma bears, spa buddies, mentors, and
prayer warriors. Thank you.

To Martani, Ben, and Lois, and in loving memory of
Dennis. You've been a part of my family for so long.
Thank you for giving me hope, I pray this book can return
a small bit of hope to your arms.

And at last, in memory of Ryan and pink skies.
You're the dreamer we lost too soon.

as a thank you for reading this book & purchasing the paperback, you can download the ebook version in our store for free!

dragonbonepublishing.gumroad.com/l/thh

with code:
th7j8hv3

About The Author

R.C. Lloyd is a writer from Upstate NY, known for her first two poetry books, *Chronic Defiance* and *The Cruelty of a Door*. You can often find her lost deep in the woods or deep in a book.

If you enjoyed this collection, you might like these other titles!

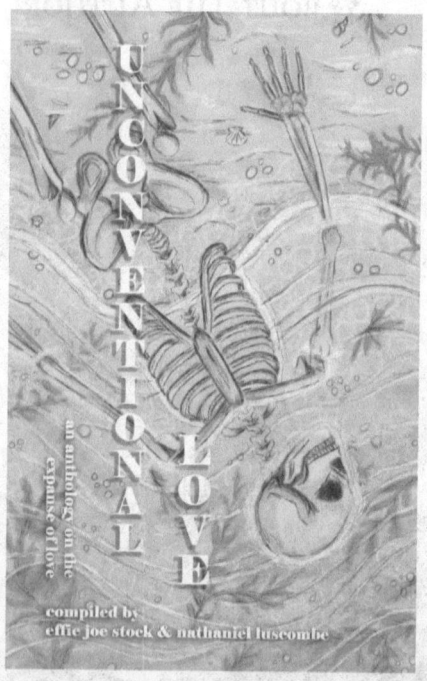

Unconventional Love
edited by Effie Joe Stock and Nathaniel Luscombe

Familial. Romantic. Platonic.

From loving your partner as a worm, to a love letter from a daughter to mother, to faun and mergirl lovers separated by culture, to a telepathic friendship nearly cast away, Unconventional Love is a collection like no other, bringing together hearts and emotions scattered across a universe so vast and an even greater love.

best cat in show

by sage evergreen

A TELL ALL STORY FROM THE FIVE YEAR CHAMPION OF THE TRADITIONAL PEDIGREE: PENNSYLVANIA COMPETITION

"the thing about being a cat bred for competition // is that your life is no longer your own..."

sage evergreen's debut collection follows a cream point birman through the hoops and jumps of competition, exploring the way the body holds on to trauma, training, and toxic upbringings.

will the wondercat break free? is there time to be a housepet, after everything?

Tending Clay; Unearthing Stars
by MJ Anthony

Today I am learning // to take anxiety by the hand // and teach this trembling, fragile beast // that we are (and yet will be) // okay.

In their debut collection, MJ Anthony navigates a complicated web of intersecting topics such as complex trauma, neurodiversity, lasting illness, and practicing self-love in a body long-alienated from you. Alongside the reader, the author combs tangles into threads and weaves them into a gentler future, reunifying selves and stories both old and new.

Part hurting, part healing, and wholly original, *Tending Clay; Unearthing Stars* is a love letter to everyone living with a broken body or a troubled mind.